Community History

Printed in Mexico

ISBN-13: 978-0-15-352799-9
ISBN-10: 0-15-352799-4

5 6 7 8 9 10   050   11 10 09 08 07

SCHOOL PUBLISHERS

Visit *The Learning Site!* www.harcourtschool.com

Communities Through Time

READ TO FIND OUT **How do communities change and stay the same?**

All communities change. They also stay the same. Many old buildings are still used. But they have new things in them. Some kinds of work are the same. However, they are done in new ways.

Chicago long ago

Most changes happen slowly. Places grow. People tear down old buildings. They put up new ones. They build roads.

Some changes happen quickly. In 1871, a fire burned most of the buildings in Chicago, Illinois. At that time, many buildings were made of wood. After the fire, the buildings were built again. Now Chicago is a large city.

READING CHECK ᛠ SEQUENCE **How do communities change and stay the same?**

Chicago today

People Bring Changes

READ TO FIND OUT **How have people changed communities?**

People change communities with inventions. **Inventions** are things that are made for the first time. Trains were inventions. They caused changes. Trains were a fast way to move people and goods. They joined towns, and the towns grew.

Trains were new inventions.

People change communities with ideas. People work to make sure everyone has the same **rights**, or freedoms.

Dr. Martin Luther King, Jr., worked for rights. In his time, African Americans did not have the same rights as white people. African American children could not go to school with white children. Now they can.

`READING CHECK` **SUMMARIZE How have people changed communities?**

Dr. Martin Luther King, Jr., worked for equal rights.

Inventions in Communities

READ TO FIND OUT **What are some inventions that have changed our lives?**

Inventions add to technology. **Technology** is the tools people can use every day. They change the way people live.

Long ago, letters took a long time to reach people. The telephone helped people communicate faster.

Alexander Graham Bell invented the telephone.

The Wright brothers and their Model A airplane

Inventions have helped people go places, too. In 1903, Orville Wright flew the first powered airplane. Now airplanes fly people and goods everywhere.

Inventions have also changed homes. Television and radio bring us the news. We use many helpful kitchen inventions.

READING CHECK **SUMMARIZE What are some inventions that have changed our lives?**

7

Communities Long Ago

READ TO FIND OUT What inventions from long ago do we use today?

People today use the inventions of people who lived long ago. The Sumerians invented the wheel. They also used symbols to write. The Chinese invented paper.

Sumerian writing

Roman citizens met in a forum.

Governments were thought of long ago, too. Athens, Greece, had the first democracy about 2,500 years ago. In a **democracy**, the citizens decide things.

The citizens of Rome chose leaders. The leaders decided things for the people. This was another form of government.

READING CHECK SUMMARIZE **What inventions from long ago do we use today?**

9

The First Communities

READ TO FIND OUT Who made the first communities in North America?

Native Americans made the first communities in North America. Native Americans once lived in every part of what is now the United States. They lived in groups.

Native Americans in different places ate different foods. They wore different kinds of clothing. They also lived in different kinds of homes.

Native American Groups

INUIT
MAKAH
CHINOOK
ATHABASKAN
YUPIK
INUIT
ALEUT
PACIFIC OCEAN
0 400 Miles
0 400 Kilometers

Lake Superior   CANADA   PENOBSCOT
YAKIMA
NEZ PERCE   CROW   MANDAN   CHIPPEWA
SIOUX
Lake Huron   Lake Ontario   WAMPANOAG
SIOUX   SAUK   Lake Michigan   Lake Erie   MASSACHUSET
CHEYENNE   FOX   IROQUOIS
HOOPA   PAIUTE   SHOSHONE   PAWNEE   IOWAY   DELAWARE
PACIFIC OCEAN   POMO   SHOSHONE   UTE   ARAPAHO   MIAMI   POWHATAN
ILLINOIS
PAIUTE   MISSOURI
KAW   SHAWNEE
YOKUTS   OSAGE   TUSCARORA
PACIFIC OCEAN   CHUMASH   HOPI   APACHE   KIOWA   CHEROKEE
0 100 Miles   NAVAJO   QUAPAW   ATLANTIC OCEAN
0 100 Kilometers   YUMA (QUECHAN)   PUEBLO   CHICKASAW   CREEK
TOHONO O'ODHAM   APACHE   COMANCHE   CADDO
CHOCTAW
NATCHEZ
N
W   E
S

Map Key
— Present-day border

MEXICO

0 200 400 Miles
0 200 400 Kilometers

TIMUCUA
CALUSA
Gulf of Mexico

An Iroquois longhouse

The people in a group used the same land. They lived in the same way. Groups who lived near forests used wood to build homes. Groups in places with few trees used mud bricks or grasses to build homes.

Some groups moved from place to place. These groups hunted. They also gathered plants. Other groups stayed in one place and farmed.

READING CHECK ☼ **SEQUENCE Who made the first communities in North America?**

Building Communities

READ TO FIND OUT **Why did Europeans build communities in North America?**

Christopher Columbus sailed from Spain to North America in 1492. Soon other Europeans came to the Americas. Some wanted land or riches. Others wanted to spread their religion. A **religion** is a belief system.

Christopher Columbus came to the Americas with three sailing ships.

Jamestown was the first lasting English community in North America.

The French came to North America. They went along the Mississippi River. They wanted a good place to trade for furs. They started a trading community. It became St. Louis.

In 1607, the English came to what is now Virginia. They started Jamestown. They wanted to find riches and a way to the Pacific Ocean. Some wanted to spread their religion, too.

READING CHECK **MAIN IDEA AND DETAILS Why did Europeans build communities in North America?**

Fighting for Freedom

READ TO FIND OUT **Who fought for our freedom?**

By the 1700s, Britain ruled 13 colonies in what is now the United States. A **colony** is a settlement ruled by a country that is far away. People who live in a colony are called colonists. Britain made laws that the colonists felt were not fair. They wanted their own laws.

The Boston Tea Party

The Constitution was written during the Constitutional Convention.

The colonists decided to fight for their freedom. Leaders of the colonies wrote the Declaration of Independence in 1776. It told why the colonists wanted freedom. It said the colonies were a new country—the United States of America.

The Revolutionary War ended in 1783. The Americans had won their freedom. In 1787, leaders wrote the Constitution. It told how the new government would work.

READING CHECK **MAIN IDEA AND DETAILS** **Who fought for our freedom?**

Franklin and Jefferson

"We hold these truths to be self-evident, that all men are created equal, that they are endowed by their Creator with certain unalienable Rights, that among these are Life, Liberty, and the pursuit of Happiness."

— the Declaration of Independence

Time

1700

1775 Jefferson and Franklin represent their states in the Continental Congress

1776 Jefferson and Franklin, and John Adams draft the Declaration of Independence

Thomas Jefferson and Benjamin Franklin wrote the Declaration of Independence in 1776. These men were different in some ways. Jefferson was from Virginia. He owned land. He was rich. Franklin had to work from the time he was ten.

Both these men loved the land where they were born. They thought it should be a country. They thought it should have its own government. The United States of America began with their help.

1830

1787 Franklin signs the Constitution of the United States

1801 Jefferson becomes third President of the United States

Growth and Change

READ TO FIND OUT How did the United States grow and change?

In 1803, President Thomas Jefferson bought land from the French. After that, the United States stretched to the Rocky Mountains. President Jefferson asked Meriwether Lewis and William Clark to see what the land was like. He wanted them to find a way to the Pacific Ocean.

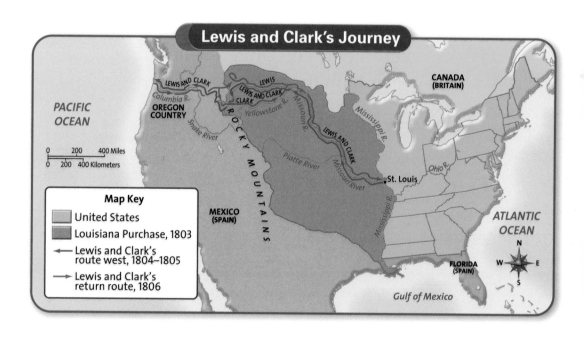

Lewis and Clark's Journey

PACIFIC OCEAN

0 200 400 Miles
0 200 400 Kilometers

CANADA (BRITAIN)

LEWIS AND CLARK
Columbia R.
OREGON COUNTRY
LEWIS
LEWIS AND CLARK
CLARK
Yellowstone R.
Snake River
Missouri R.
Mississippi R.
LEWIS AND CLARK
Platte River
Missouri River
Ohio R.
St. Louis

ROCKY MOUNTAINS

MEXICO (SPAIN)

Mississippi R.

ATLANTIC OCEAN

Map Key

United States
Louisiana Purchase, 1803
Lewis and Clark's route west, 1804–1805
Lewis and Clark's return route, 1806

FLORIDA (SPAIN)

Gulf of Mexico

N
W   E
S

Some people moved across the country in covered wagons.

Lewis and Clark made maps. They wrote about their trip. Their work helped other people move across the country in the 1800s.

By 1869, people could take trains across the country. The United States kept growing. Ships brought many people to the United States from other countries.

READING CHECK 🖐 SEQUENCE **How did the United States grow and change?**

The Corps of Discovery

Background The Lewis and Clark trip lasted more than two years. Lewis and Clark wrote about the people and the land.

MAPS

Lewis and Clark used this map for their trip.

PEACE MEDAL

Lewis and Clark gave Peace Medals to the Native Americans.

CAPTAIN CLARK'S JOURNAL

Each day, Clark wrote what he had done and seen.

A NOOTKA HAT

Lewis and Clark collected this hat from Native Americans they met.

❶ Why did the map have few details?

❷ What might Clark's journal tell about the land he saw?

Activity 1

Match the word to its meaning.

rights   religion

colony   inventions

democracy   technology

1. things that are made for the first time

2. all of the tools people can use every day

3. freedoms

4. a settlement ruled by a country that is far away

5. a person's belief system

6. a kind of government in which the citizens decide things

Activity 2

Look at the list of vocabulary words. Categorize the words in a chart like the one below. Then use a dictionary to learn the definitions of the words you do not know.

pioneer	revolution	suffrage	republic
language	democracy	constitution	empire
independence	trade	modern	tax
century	decade	vote	port
settlement	oral history	claim	settler
patriotism	civil rights	territory	freedom
immigrant	explorer	equality	right
invention	religion	continuity	slavery
engineer	conflict	civil war	ancient
civilization	President	colony	slogan
amendment	technology	shelter	

		I Know	Sounds Familiar	Don't Know
○	pioneer			✓
	century		✓	
	explorer	✓		

Sequence Who sailed to North America in 1492?

Vocabulary

1. What is a **democracy**?

Recall

2. What did Dr. Martin Luther King, Jr., do?

3. What are two inventions that helped people go places?

4. Why did Europeans come to the Americas?

Critical Thinking

5. How might the United States be different if Americans had lost the Revolutionary War?

Activity

Make a List Make a list of five inventions. Then pick the one you like best. Write a sentence to explain the reason for your choice.

Photo credits Front Cover Larry Lefever/Grant Heilman Photography; 2 New York Public Library Picture Collection; 3 Adam Jones/Getty Images; 5 Bob Fitch/Stock Photo; 6 Bettmann/CORBIS; 7 Underwood & Underwood/CORBIS; 8 Réunion des Musées Nationaux/Art Resource; 11 Nathan Benn/Corbis; 12 Private Collection, Index/Bridgeman Art Library; 13 Richard T. Nowitz/Corbis; 14 Bettmann/CORBIS; 15 The Granger Collection, New York; 16 The Granger Collection, New York; 17 The Granger Collection, New York; 20 Geography and Map Division/The Library of Congress; 21 (tr) The Granger Collection, New York; 21 (tl) Oregon Historical Society; 21 (bl) Erich Lessing/Art Resource, NY

STRAND
History
WORD COUNT
942
GENRE
Nonfiction
LEVEL
See TG or go Online

GO online Harcourt Leveled
Readers Online Database
www.eharcourtschool.com

ISBN-13: 978-0-15-352799-9
ISBN-10: 0-15-352799-4

90000 >

9 780153 527999

Harcourt
SCHOOL PUBLISHERS